THE VA

A VETERAN/PATIENT/ VOLUNTEER

M E M O I R

RICK BUTLER

THE VA
A VETERAN/PATIENT/ VOLUNTEER MEMOIR

This book is a work of fiction. It is based, however, on Rick's interactions with the VA and his time as a combat paratrooper in Vietnam. The VA interactions included VA patients, volunteers, healthcare workers, and healthcare services. Any similarity of characters or events in this book to real persons or happenings is purely coincidental and is not meant to injure, slander, incriminate or defame anyone.

Edited by: Maya Butler

iUniverse books may be ordered through booksellers or by contacting:

iUniverse
1663 Liberty Drive
Bloomington, IN 47403
www.iuniverse.com
844-349-9409

Because of the dynamic nature of the Internet, any web addresses or links contained in this book may have changed since publication and may no longer be valid. The views expressed in this work are solely those of the author and do not necessarily reflect the views of the publisher, and the publisher hereby disclaims any responsibility for them.

Any people depicted in stock imagery provided by Getty Images are models, and such images are being used for illustrative purposes only. Certain stock imagery © Getty Images.

ISBN: 978-1-6632-3283-0 (sc)
ISBN: 978-1-6632-3647-0 (e)

Print information available on the last page.

iUniverse rev. date: 02/22/2022

ACKNOWLEDGEMENTS

The Veterans – a special thanks to all the veterans that I have interacted with at the VA. These men and women have honorably served our country and it has been my honor to get to know these true Americans

My Fellow Volunteers – have been an inspiration to me as I have seen them assist veteran patients treating them with the utmost dignity and respect. These volunteers are very special, giving people who help us meet our commitment to the vets.

The VA Health Care workers – are wonderful – providing outstanding health care to our veterans with the honor and respect they have earned and deserve

Maya Butler – who not only edited this book but also provided guidance and input to these writings. As my grand-daughter and a fellow volunteer she has been an inspiration for me to write and complete this book. Thank you Maya!

CHAPTER 1

THE BEGINNING – ARMY ETS/ EARLY OUT FOR COLLEGE

As I was getting ready for ETS (estimated time served, aka getting out of Army), I was given my ETS physical. This is a standard procedure for everyone getting out of the service. For the most part, the results were pretty good. Still, there were some areas of concern: combat fatigue, recurring malaria, and damage to my hearing. Well, maybe not so good...

As for combat fatigue, I was diagnosed with this at the end of my one-year deployment to Vietnam. I was a combat paratrooper (airborne infantry) and was engaged in combat operations throughout my deployment. I also was one of our point men – the lead person in combat maneuvers being the first soldier in harm's way. As a point man, I would go out by myself two or three hundred yards and then stop to have others link up with me. The idea being if there is an ambush, etc., only one person would be involved initially to minimize our casualties. As it turned out, all of our point men were killed, captured, or wounded – all except me. Things happened all around me, but I was lucky. And as you might suspect, I have survivor's guilt in spades.

As for malaria, I was not aware of having a malaria attack in Vietnam. Although, during one of my R&Rs Rs (R&R stands for rest and rehabilitation – a 5 to 7 day break from the war spent in Tokyo, Bangkok, etc.). I had a fever one night that broke, and my sweat caused all of the bedding to be soaked. But it went away, and I didn't think much about it. However, after being back from Vietnam for five months and stationed at Fort Knox, I came home from work one day sick and I laid down on the couch with my field jacket on. It was 85 degrees and humid with no air conditioning, but I was cold. My wife Judy went and got one of our neighbors, who had also been in Vietnam. He took one look at me and said I had malaria, and he was going to take me to the hospital. I said no, I didn't have malaria in Vietnam, so I don't have it now. He told me either he would take me to the hospital or call an ambulance. He took me to the hospital, where they confirmed his diagnosis of malaria. I was the first malaria case they ever had at Fort Knox, so every Dr. in the hospital wanted to see me - a malaria patient. I felt like I was an animal in a zoo as they paraded by me. For the first week, I did not get better – having temperatures between 104 and 106. I was having hallucinations, and they were giving me cold showers. At one point, they caught me trying to get in bed with another patient. They asked me what I was doing, and I said I was getting in bed with my new wife. And they gave me another cold shower. This may sound kind of funny, but they were concerned about brain damage from the fevers. Then they realized I had two different types of malaria, both of which were recurring. Each type of malaria required different medications. So, once they started treating me for both, I started getting better. After two weeks in the hospital, I was discharged and given a 45-day convalescent leave because I was as weak as a kitten. To this day they still say I have recurring malaria in my blood but at a dormant state. I can never donate blood.

With respect to my hearing, we were exposed to tremendous explosions from automatic weapon fire, mortar rounds, rockets, hand grenades and artillery. One time we were in a tunnel when a hand grenade went off. Half of us had blood coming out of our ears. I had no blood, but I couldn't hear anything for two days.

The Army told me that I would be awarded disabilities for malaria and combat fatigue. But I needed to take more hearing tests, and it would delay me getting out of the Army. I said I was getting an early out for college, and I couldn't be delayed as my classes were starting. They said okay if I would sign a release on my hearing, I would not have the follow-up and could get out of the Army on time. I agreed and signed the release. And to this day I still have significant hearing loss.

Shortly after I got out of the Army, I got a letter from the VA saying they were awarding me disability for my combat fatigue (20%) and malaria (10%). There were some rather minimal disability payments related to those assessments. They also said that these areas would be reassessed periodically and would be subject to change. As it turned out, I never have had another documented recurrence of malaria. Although I periodically have night sweats, which I've been told can be related to my malaria. As for my combat fatigue, I was a mess during the year and a half I spent at Fort Knox. Of course, in their infinite wisdom, the Army did not treat me for my combat fatigue – no counseling, no nothing. I guess they figured removing me from combat was enough. Well, not quite. My nightmares were frequent, all too realistic and haunting. They scared my wife, Judy, a lot. But ultimately, the nightmares became less frequent, and my nervousness subsided at least to some degree.

CHAPTER 2

DON'T TALK ABOUT VIETNAM

After the Army, I went to a college located outside of my home state. I had asked the Army if I was to be considered a resident of any state I went to, being I had no state residency for the past three years. They said yes and that I would then pay in-state tuition.

Well, I should have known better than to ask the Army about civilian life. My first visit to my college told me I was still considered a resident of my home state coming out of the military. Because I was a resident of my home state going in – so the same going out. Of course, this meant 'out of state tuition' – three times the resident rate.

Somehow, the governor of my relocated state had gotten word that I was coming out of the Army and was moving to his state. His office sent me a letter thanking me for my service and welcoming me. It also said if I ever need his help, I should contact him. So, I did, and his office said they would have one of his staff follow-up on this. After a couple of days, I was told that the law clearly supports their position and that I would become a resident after living here for one year. I barely was able to scrape up the money for tuition and had I not; I would have had to go back in the Army to finish up my time. Welcome home – Vietnam Veteran.

Out of state tuition was hard to take, but the GI Bill was not. I applied for my VA benefits from the GI Bill and was awarded them. They came in the form of monthly payments during the time I was a full-time college student. These payments covered a good portion of my 1st year out of state tuition and more than covered my subsequent in-state tuition. They did little toward room and board (our living expenses). But to say there is no way I could have attended college without the GI Bill is a gross understatement.

9

My first visit to the student union for coffee taught me a big lesson. Don't tell people you are a Vietnam veteran. As I was invited to join a group of people who were having a discussion, I learned it was about Vietnam. My college was a conservative campus, so there were no demonstrations about the Vietnam War. But there were discussions, and I got into one. I told them what I had done (Army combat paratrooper) and my perspective on the war. I said me and my buddies were disappointed that they would not let us end the war. With our firepower from the air force, helicopters, artillery, and Navy destroyers and even the New Jersey a battleship with 16-inch guns, we could have marched on Hanoi with our Army & Marines and flattened Hanoi within six months. With North Vietnam defeated the resupplies to the Viet Cong in South Vietnam would have ended and they would have ceased to be any significant threat. But our government was afraid of the reactions from Russia and China.

Well, this group I was talking with did not see it that way. They felt we had no business being there in the first place and that I had no business fighting in that war. They were not only against the war but also against the vets who had fought there. They did not spit on me and call me a baby killer like certain others were known to do. But it was clear; I was not thought of well, respected, or honored for having fought in that war. I learned right then and there not to tell people I was a Vietnam veteran and to keep my mouth shut. Welcome home, Vietnam veteran.

I also realized that my definition of friendship had changed. My buddies in Vietnam would do anything for you, including fighting to their death if it came to that. I saw guys risk their lives again and again to rescue/help their wounded buddies. And yet as I interacted with my friends at home, most everything seemed superficial and unimportant. We had a saying Vietnam – 'don't mean nothin'.' This meant if it wasn't life or death, it didn't really matter. I tried to explain some of this to a couple of friends, but they couldn't relate to what I said. They didn't get it. And I couldn't blame them as you really had to have been there and experienced the horrors of war to understand. I had to be content with what I deemed superficial friendships and not try to explain why I felt different from so many others. I felt alone and isolated. So once again, I learned to keep my mouth shut about Vietnam – a recurrent and unhealthy theme that ground me to silence.

CHAPTER 3

VA – STAYING IN TOUCH

Although I had the GI – Bill to help me with my college expenses that was not nearly enough, especially that first year with out of state tuition. Judy was working full time as a bank teller, and I got a job as a bartender in a supper club. In my first year, I worked 40 to 48 hours a week and went to school full time. My typical work week was working from 5 pm to 1 am five to six days a week, Often l would have an 8:00 am class, and I had great difficulty staying awake as evidenced by my notes abruptly stopping with a line down the page as I fell to sleep,

This schedule affected my grades as my first quarter was a 2.0 as I worked 48 hours a week. Then I cut back to 40 hours, and my grades improved. To say I was busy was an understatement, to say the least. But I was somewhat used to long hours. In combat, we were constantly moving in search of the enemy. Every day we would move and then set up a perimeter late in the day and dig our foxholes. At night we had to pull guard duty at our foxhole – each of us for two hours. We would stay out in the field (triple canopy jungles or rice paddies) executing combat operations 30 to 45 days in a row and then get a five day stand down (rest) in our fire support base, which was carved out of the jungle. But even there, we still had to perform guard duty on the perimeter. There was very little rest or sleep in combat.

I did not take the summers off as I went to both summer school sessions, trying to finish my accounting degree as soon as possible. And I further cut back my work to 32 hours a week. This allowed me to carry more credits, and my grades continued to improve. Again, I cut my hours this time to 24 hours/week and took student loans as well. My last year, I quit work and carried nearly 20 credits each quarter to finish my degree in 3 and ¼ years (my college was on the quarter system vs semester).

During my senior year, I met with my counselor to discuss what I needed to graduate. She told me that I had received an extraordinary amount of ROTC (Reserve Officer Training Course) credits for three years in the Army including my deployment to Vietnam as a combat paratrooper. I only needed to take one ROTC class to graduate from ROTC to go back into the Army as a 2nd Lieutenant (officer pay grade 1 – the lowest). I said, "No, thanks." I was a buck sergeant E-5 (enlisted pay grade 5), and they wanted to promote me to Staff Sergeant E-6 (enlisted pay grade 6). But I wouldn't sign a document called 'Intent to Re-enlist.' So basically, I was an E-6. Why would I want to go back in as a 2nd Lieutenant O-1? I was totally done with the Army.

I also maxed out my student loans, which put us in dire financial straits my last quarter. Fortunately, Judy got a 25 lb turkey for Thanksgiving from her bank. And we pretty much ate turkey for almost every meal between Thanksgiving and Christmas. I got job offers from 4 of the eight big national CPA firms and accepted a job with one of them. They wanted me to start work on January 2nd, but I asked if I could start on December 26th. They asked me why, and I explained that we were running out of the 25-pound Thanksgiving turkey my wife got from her bank. They seemed shocked, but they understood and said, of course, I could start on the 26th.

I was an auditor and I passed the CPA exam and became a CPA. Again, this was a demanding job with a lot of travel and overtime. Still, I was used to working hard, and the pay was unbelievable. It felt like we went from rags to riches. We were such paupers in college, and I became a well-paid 'up and coming professional.' In fact, we were able to pay off all my student loans within 2½ years.

The other thing that took place around this time was the purchase of our first home. We looked for a modest home and found what had initially been an old farmhouse that the suburbs had grown up around. We had very little savings as we had been paying off my student loans. But we were able to buy this house with a zero down GI loan. And our payments were very close to what we had been paying in rent. So once again, the VA had come through for me – a recurrent and welcome theme.

With my extreme schedule and my new career, my Vietnam experience faded away, at least to a certain degree, with the nightmares and flashbacks diminishing as well. Periodically during college, I got letters from the VA, asking me to come in for appointments to reassess my disabilities. I had not had any more malaria attacks, so they reduced my disability ratings with malaria rated at 0, and my combat fatigue 10%.

After working as a CPA for nearly three years, the VA called me back in for an appointment with a psychiatrist to reassess my combat fatigue. I went to that appointment wearing my best three-piece suit, white shirt, and tie.

The doctor introduced himself and asked me how I was doing. I told him I was cured. My combat fatigue stuff was over, and I was doing great. I told him I had graduated from college and was a CPA working for a large national CPA firm. Student loans paid off, and I was good. I told him I didn't want my disability anymore, and they should give the money to someone else who needed it. He seemed taken aback. He couldn't believe what I was saying. He said he had some questions for me before any decision on my disability could be made. I said okay and thought I could easily answer his questions and be done with all of this.

Well, not so. He started asking me some pretty generic questions about my Vietnam experience. I calmly began answering his questions. But the questions became more pointed at my combat experience, asking me why I thought I ended up with combat fatigue. His questions triggered memories, guilt, and shame that bothered me. I tried answering them but began crying. Soon I was sobbing and shaking – totally overwhelmed as the blocked horrible memories flooded back to me. He quit asking me questions, sat down next to me, and put his hand on my shoulder.

As I settled down, he told me what now seemed very obvious. - I was not cured. And I never would be without a lot of therapy. He said I could not give back my disability, and it would be left as before. He offered to see me for therapy. I was still upset and confused, so I told him no thanks. He gave me his card and asked that I call him back if I changed my mind.

I walked in there thinking I was cured and walked out in a daze, hoping I could push the flood gates back in place.

CHAPTER 4

PTSD

I managed to mostly close the flood gates and continued with my career. I had changed jobs and was working for a manufacturing company as an assistant controller. I got very involved in data processing as we were automating many of their manual systems. We were doing very well, making a lot of progress when our parent company hired a new MIS (Management Information Systems) Director. He was not officially my boss but he got very involved in what we were doing.

At about this time I was talking to an army buddy and he thought I might have PTSD and thought I should get it checked out. I contacted the VA's Vet Center to get an assessment. About that same time, I remember very clearly washing my car in the driveway and listening to the radio. I heard a helicopter flyover. It sounded very much like a Huey, which gave me the chills due to the large number of combat assaults we did with Hueys in Vietnam. At that same time, a news report came over the radio announcing that China was staging a number of troops along their border with Vietnam for a possible invasion. China and Vietnam had border clashes at the time. I got this bizarre feeling about wanting to become a mercenary and fight Vietnam again, this time with China. This feeling became very strong, which I knew wasn't right, but I could not help my feelings. I started thinking more and more about Vietnam. I was also having trouble with my new boss at work. He was messing in my stuff, trying to tell me to do things that didn't make sense, and I did not like that.

When I went to the Vet Center, they hooked me up with a psychiatrist who would talk with me to determine if I had PTSD and what to do about it. I was concerned when I found out this guy had never been to Vietnam, never been in combat, or even in the service. I couldn't imagine how such a person could understand my problems related to Vietnam. He asked me what bothered me most about Vietnam. No one had ever asked me that question before. I thought about it for a while, and I told him that many of my friends were wounded or killed, including one of my best friends, Ray who was killed with 16 days left.

I felt guilty about surviving and felt a part of me died in Vietnam. I had trouble relating to people since my return. I felt like my whole life didn't 'mean nothing.' I felt no one cared about what I did in Vietnam. I felt abandoned and alone. And that no-one could help me. My psychiatrist listened to me, and towards the end, tears rolled down his cheeks, and he told me I was wrong because he cared about what I did in Vietnam, and he would help me. I thought it was strange because psychiatrists were not supposed to cry. But somehow, this convinced me that he did understand, and he would help.

My psychiatrist thought I might benefit from group therapy. I went to one session and quickly decided I did not like it. When I would speak and say what was bothering me, the other guys said they had not gone through half of what I had and thought they shouldn't be having any problems. This bothered me because everything is relative. I did not want them to feel like that. I told my psychiatrist what had happened and why I didn't like it. He understood completely and thanked me for feeling that way for the good of the guys.

I went through a ton of counseling sessions. But I was still feeling desperate and all alone. My psychiatrist thought I had unsettled business about Vietnam, especially related to Ray. I had tried to write his Mom from Vietnam about Ray's death, but the Army wouldn't give me her address. So, I wrote President Reagan (attn Elizabeth Dole). Within a week, I got a call from a colonel who said President Reagan had asked him to help me. Ultimately, they got a letter forwarded to Ray's mom from me. It came back undeliverable – addressee unknown. At least I had tried.

And I needed to try because Ray had met so much to me. Ray befriended me when I got to Vietnam. This was so important because, as a new guy, you had no idea how to react in combat. Whether it was sniper fire, booby traps, being mortared, an ambush or a fire fight, you didn't know what to do. And freezing up or doing the wrong thing will get you hurt or killed in a heartbeat. Most of the causalities of the Vietnam War happened to new guys. So, Ray taking me under his wing and showing me the ropes probably saved my life or at least spared me from being wounded. Ray was always next to me and would show or tell me immediately what to do. Ray was a very small, quiet, Hispanic guy from New Mexico who got care packages from home that included tequila with a worm in it and hot peppers. He was far different from me – a tall, white guy from a small town 35 miles from downtown Chicago. And my care packages from home mostly included spam, Heinz 57 sauce, and cookies. But somehow, we connected. Ray was a very nice guy who loved to laugh and joke around. He was a point man extraordinaire and was revered as being fearless and clearly one of our best point men. He also protected me from some of the seasoned combat guys who liked to pick on new guys. When a seasoned guy would start to pick on me, Ray would say in a soft voice 'leave him alone' and they immediately would stop. Ray was totally respected, and although he was a nice, quiet guy, when the shit hit the fan, he became a fierce warrior. Nobody messed with Ray – nobody.

As Ray started teaching me to walk point, I knew he had been wounded twice while on point. I asked him why he wasn't afraid to walk point as he had been wounded twice. He said it was simple – there was a rule that if you are wounded three times, they take you out of combat and send you home.

Well, Ray did go home with his third purple heart as I placed him in a body bag and put him on a helicopter that took him out of combat and towards home. This was during operation Cochise (some of our combat operations were given nicknames – this one was Cochise), which unfortunately led to our platoon being wiped out. Ray was on point and was going slow because there were booby traps in the area. He was told two or three times to hurry up which he finally did. And then I heard and felt a tremendous explosion followed by screams. I knew it was bad. Ray had stepped on a booby trapped 105 artillery round. This not only killed him but also the dog and dog handler which were right up with Ray on point. Two or three other guys were wounded with one nearly having his arm blown off. This was my worst day in Vietnam and the first and only time I cried. I couldn't believe it; it wasn't fair. And after the last of the medi-vac helicopters took Ray and the other dead and wounded away, they said saddle up, and off we went as if nothing had happened. But something had happened. My best friend was killed by his third purple heart with 16 days left in Vietnam. And this probably caused me to continue to walk point and to become somewhat fearless to honor Ray. Someone had to do it because Ray was gone, and he had given it his all…

I then decided I needed to contact my other best friend, Mike. Mike, Ray, and I all walked point, and I knew if there was anyone I needed to hook up with, it was Mike. I wrote him a letter telling him how much trouble I was having and that I needed to see him. I mailed it to his mom's address, which I still had. I remember very clearly the fall evening I was outside raking leaves. Judy came out and said I had a call from California, and I knew it was Mike. But it wasn't, it was Mike's brother. He said he didn't know how to tell me this, but Mike was killed in a hang-gliding accident three years before. Mike's brother had been in Vietnam, too, as a helicopter pilot. He talked to me for a long time and offered to come to my home to see me. He said Mike had been having a lot of problems like me before he died. I thanked him but said no. I was crushed – my last hope was gone. It was like being back on point again – all alone and there seemed to be no one left to link up with me.

I was so messed up I was even talking to a recruiter, thinking that going back in the service might get me closer to people I could relate to. But I was a little smarter this time and wanted to be a finance officer being I had an accounting degree, was a CPA and had worked for nearly five years for a big national CPA firm. And, of course, I was only one class from graduating from ROTC which would have gotten me into the Army as a 2nd lieutenant (O-1). I wanted to go in as a Major (O-4 and three ranks above a 2nd lieutenant). He laughed and said 2nd lieutenant, and I had to retake basic training. I said, no way. I had been running marathons and had been in combat, so the last thing I needed was basic training. And again, I said Major. He finally agreed to no basic and 1st Lieutenant (O-2). – one rank above 2nd lieutenant. About that time, Judy told my psychiatrist about the recruiter. I'm not sure if it was Judy or my psychiatrist, but someone talked to the recruiter, and all of a sudden, all that talk was over.

I told Judy that I was scared, all alone, and didn't know what to do. I decided I would talk to a friend of mine who had played basketball with me on an over 30 team and was a pastor. I told him I was having psychological problems related to Vietnam and needed to talk to him. I went to his church, sat down, and told him what was going on. About trying to send a letter to Ray's mom and what had happened with Mike. I was crying, and I looked up, and he was crying. He took me in his arms, and we both cried. He said, 'I don't know what to say other than to ask God to give you peace, Rick.' And then we held hands, and he said the prayer. I can't say that God answered this prayer immediately. But still, I knew there were at least two people (beyond my family) who cared what I had done in Vietnam and wanted to help me – my psychiatrist and my pastor friend. And also, I knew there was God. God was with me when I walked point in Vietnam. He saved me then, and I thought maybe he would save me again. And I have thanked God many times for my psychiatrist who truly saved me. I believe God sent him to me. He pulled me up out of a bottomless pit. And after two to three years of counseling – not only me but Judy was involved in a lot of it as well, I not only continued to function but got better…

CHAPTER 5

173D REUNIONS / FLASHBACKS

I changed jobs taking a job as a Corporate Accounting Manager at the newspaper. This was a good thing because it got me away from my boss, who was still giving me trouble. As it turned out, one of the administrative ladies at the newspaper that I interacted with at times somehow came to find out that I was a Vietnam veteran. She asked me what unit I was with, and I told her the 173d Airborne Brigade. She said, 'no way – my husband was with the 173d'. Not the same battalion or even the same year but still the 173d. She asked me if I had gone to any of the reunions. I said no, and I didn't even know about them. She said there was one coming up in a couple of months about a hundred miles south of us. She said she would get the information on the reunion and give it to me. I said okay, but I wasn't sure if I would go as I had a very rough time with PTSD and wasn't sure if this would be good. I got the information about the reunion and started thinking about it.

I talked to Judy about it saying I had been doing very well for quite some time and was concerned this could stir things up again. Judy agreed but also said how good it would be if you met back up with some of your buddies. I waffled back and forth for a week then I finally decided to sign up and send the $25 fee. And even though I enrolled, I could still choose not to go.

The night before, I had pretty much decided to go but still left an out for the next morning or even after getting to the reunion if it didn't feel right. I left in the morning. After arriving at the reunion, there was a reception desk, and I checked in. I acknowledged it was my first reunion to which the greeters yelled out, 'we've got a new one.' Everyone stopped what they were doing and clapped for me. This was feeling good – not a mistake.

They told me to sign one of the sign-up sheets that corresponded to my battalion and to look at the names of those attending. I looked through the names and found one I recognized – Smitty. He was in our platoon in the other squad. He was one of our point men, like me, and he was very good. Not as good as our best point man, Ray, who taught me to walk point, but still very good.

A week after Ray was killed; Smitty took his squad out for an ambush when they were ambushed. It was really bad. Jimmy got killed, another was blinded, and two others wounded. Smitty called in on the radio and said to 'come and get them – everybody is dead.' We went out and got them carrying Smitty and the others who couldn't walk. Smitty was shot in the leg and kept saying he had a million-dollar wound and was going home. They brought in a couple of medi-vac helicopters to take away the dead and the wounded. That was the last time I saw Smitty.

At the reunion I asked around if anybody knew where Smitty was. Someone said he was out in the road as they were lining up for a parade. I started looking through the guys for Smitty, and then I saw him. As he walked toward me, he was limping badly. But when he got to me, he hugged me and lifted me off the ground. We both had tears running down our cheeks. Someone asked if this was the first time we've met since Vietnam. Smitty said, 'yes, and Rick carried me out of the jungle after I was blown up and saved my life.' It was great seeing Smitty again. He told me his million-dollar wound almost killed him. His bullet wound to his leg had hit an artery. It was so dark we hadn't seen all the blood. He also had a lot of shrapnel in his back. He nearly bled out in the helicopter, went into a coma for two weeks, and was in the hospital for six months. I told him that after his squad got messed up so bad, they considered our platoon was wiped out. I said we went from 25 men to 7 of us left. Smitty got this terrified look on his face. He said he hadn't known that, and that made three platoons that Smitty had been in that were wiped out - unbelievable. The first two were only a few months before I got to Vietnam.

I saw Smitty at several 173d reunions. One was in Dallas, Texas, where we also met up with another guy from our company. He was not in our platoon, but I remembered him, and he knew me as well. He said he remembered right after I first got there. We were attached to a mechanized unit, and we were in armored personnel carriers (APCs) when we caught a whole bunch of NVA (North Vietnamese Army) soldiers out in a big open rice paddy. We literally mowed them down with the APCs 50 caliber machine guns. Many of the bodies were nearly cut in half, and there were stacks of bodies all around like cordwood. I said, 'no, I wasn't there.' He said he definitely remembered me there. I said to Smitty I wasn't there, and Smitty looked at me, and he said I absolutely was there. And suddenly, the memory came flooding back. I could feel the bumps inside the APC and hear the loud clanking of the tracks. And then I heard the 50 caliber machine guns blasting away, and I saw the piles of bodies. I had been there but had blocked out this horrible memory. This memory overwhelmed me, and it was like it had just happened. This was the type of thing that I didn't need to remember. Your mind blocks these memories out for a reason. Unfortunately, this one came back. And it was a big-time flashback. So now I knew there was an upside and downside to these reunions.

Smitty and his wife stopped by our home a couple of times on their way to visit Smitty's mom in a nursing home in the northern part of my state. After Smitty's mom died, Smitty got sick. It was cancer from Agent Orange. It was ironic how Smitty survived three platoons being wiped out, but Vietnam was not done with him yet. Agent Orange killed Smitty. And some say, 'Vietnam is a bad gift that keeps on giving' – PTSD, Agent Orange, and for some, suicide.

Vietnam tried to kill Smitty three times as his platoons were wiped out, and it came very, very close during operation Cochise. But Vietnam and Agent Orange didn't miss this time; they finally killed Smitty. May God bless Smitty's soul…

CHAPTER 6

THE IMPORTANCE OF FAMILY

I cannot overemphasize the importance of my immediate family in helping to cope with PTSD. For me, this help started with my fiancée, Judy, who was still there when I got home from Vietnam. You don't know how many times I was told, by many different guys in Vietnam, to forget about your girl back home – she won't be there when you return. Well, they were wrong. Judy was not only there, but we were married 11 days after I got back from Vietnam. She knew things were not good for me when I got home with my recurring nightmares, flashbacks, and then malaria during our time at Fort Knox.

My Mom and Dad also knew the war had changed me as they saw many of my struggles after getting back from Vietnam. This included them visiting me at the hospital in Fort Knox when I had malaria. Having loved ones around when trying to adjust and put the war behind me was very comforting at a challenging time. Maybe that's why my PTSD symptoms did not surface in a big way for 10 or 11 years after my return from Vietnam. At my worst, I didn't care about myself anymore but thank God my family loved me, and I cared about them. I can tell you that Judy was there and involved during the therapy sessions we had over the two to three-year period I was getting treatment. Judy and I have now been married for just over 50 years. She has helped me immeasurably in my ability to cope with my PTSD. She encouraged and supported me throughout my career and personal life.

And now my adult children they have been and continue to be very supportive as well. Being able to talk about the nightmares and memories that haunt me lightens their burden and helps put them in perspective. I have spoken about Vietnam to every member of my family - not just my Mom & Dad but also my two sisters and my brother. For all of this love and support not only from my family but also from Judy's family, I am eternally grateful. I would not be here today without that.

As I said earlier, in combat your friends would do anything for you. They would risk their lives to save other wounded soldiers. And we all experienced the same horrific things: the fire-fights, the snipers, the booby traps, the ambushes, pungi-pits (sharp, poisoned bamboo stakes in camouflaged pits), the jungles, the snakes (pythons, boa constrictors, bamboo vipers - known as two-step snakes since you take two steps after being bitten and die), komodo dragons, millipedes the size of your forearm that would crawl over us as we slept on the jungle floor, Bengal tigers, elephants that were stampeded through our jungle perimeters by the NVA (North Vietnam Army), malaria-ridden mosquitoes, leeches on the jungle floor and in streams, running out of food and water – all of this. Yes, all of this. We experienced all of this together and not only became friends but brothers – brothers-in-arms. Unshakeable bonds as we were all in – all in for each other.

Some returning combat veterans with severe PTSD cannot relate to their old friends and become all alone, except for family. And for those who do not have supportive families, there often is nothing. As a patient and volunteer at the VA, I have met hospitalized guys who do not want to go home. There is nothing there for them – no family or friends – nothing. They would rather stay with other vets (the brother-hood) in the hospital with supportive nurses and Doctors. Some would intentionally fall down and hurt themselves to delay their discharge from the hospital. I met a guy in the VA hospital who told me he loved to read but couldn't because his cheater glasses were at home. I asked why he didn't have someone bring them to him. He said he had no one. I told him my wife has a number of them, and I would ask her to bring some, which she did. I took them to him, and he found a pair that worked for him to read, and he wanted to pay me. I said no. And he said, why not. I said we are brothers-in-arms, so we take care of each other. And a tear rolled down his cheek as he thanked me.

There is a lot of talk about PTSD today with returning combat veterans from the Iraq and Afghanistan wars. And I have heard it emphasized more and more - the importance of family to returning combat veterans. The chairman of the Joint Chiefs of Staff, at one point, said 'make no mistake about it, the family of veterans are serving our country immensely by the burden they gladly bear in supporting our men and women in uniform – especially those returning combatants with PTSD.'

CHAPTER 7

9/11 AND RESURGENCE OF PTSD

With 9/11 came the resurgence of my PTSD. The reason my PTSD flared up is we were attacked - different than Pearl Harbor, to be sure but attacked nonetheless. And I knew we were at war. Exactly with whom I was unsure. But war is war, and so many of my feelings about Vietnam came flooding back. We saw people jumping out of the towers to their death. Watching people die and being killed was too much like Vietnam. Had I been connected to the VA, then, as I am now through my health care and volunteering, it may have been different. I would have had my friends (brother-hood) at the VA to talk to and/or my PTSD counselors. However, I had none of this but clearly felt a need to talk with other veterans.

But in business/professional environments, veterans were few and far between. This is not surprising. Not when you realize the draft rules that put so many in the service during the '60s and early '70s. If your family *was* well-to-do and could send you to college, you got a draft deferment. If not, you were classified 1A and drafted into the Army or the Marines. I was enrolled in college but got this crazy idea of joining the Army to be a paratrooper. A lot of my buddies were going away to college, as was my girlfriend. I was enrolled in a local college, so I felt like I was being left behind. Why exactly I wanted to be a paratrooper was unclear, but it probably had something to do with all the John Wayne movies I saw as a kid that glorified paratroopers and war. Had I been smart, I could have volunteered for the draft (2 years) instead of enlisting for three years to be a paratrooper. Had I been drafted, I could have volunteered to be a paratrooper. But at 18 years old you don't always think things through. And being a paratrooper was a ticket to being a combat infantry guy and going to Vietnam in 1968. The good news is I was no longer being left behind. The bad news was Vietnam was a very long, long way from home. And, of course, it was so very different from going to college.

As a finance director, at the newspaper, I interacted mostly with senior management, and very few of these people ever were in the service as most attended college and earned degrees. If I had been closer to the newspaper's printing operations, there would have been more veterans around from the blue-collar ranks. But I was removed from them except for one electrician.

I'm not sure how I got to know this guy, but he worked in the office area. As it turned out, he was a Vietnam veteran as well and also an infantry combat guy like me. He had served with the 1st infantry division. We started talking occasionally, and our conversation started centering on 9/11. He and I both had this irrational feeling and desire to join up again to fight the enemy who had attacked us. We were both far too old to go back into the military, but the feeling was there just the same. He was not a college guy, so he was drafted into the Army for two years. My electrician friend got out of the Army right after Vietnam and had a hard time with the war protestors calling him a baby killer and being spat upon. I didn't have that problem as I was married, and Judy and I spent the last year and one half of my Army time at Fort Knox. This was a good place sheltering me from a lot of the social unrest about Vietnam. I told him about my combat fatigue and PTSD and that I was having a hard time with my bosses at work. For me, the work environment had changed to more of a 'do it and shut up' attitude, which was bothersome for me as it triggered flashbacks to Vietnam. I'm not sure if he had PTSD, as he chose not to talk much about his combat experience. I told him I went to college after the Army on the GI Bill. He told me he used the GI Bill as well for his electrician's training.

CHAPTER 8

SHUT UP AND DO IT

Toward the end of my career things had changed at work. *Before* the environment was such that you were encouraged to question things that didn't make sense. Many times, the things you were being asked to do could be done far more efficiently in a slightly different manner and still fundamentally accomplish the goal. As a senior manager and director, I knew what needed to be done. I didn't need someone hovering over me, telling me what to do, and micro-managing me.

This 'shut up and do it' atmosphere was unhealthy for me. This type of direction causes me to flashback to a horrible experience I had in Vietnam. We were in the lowlands with terrain of tree lines, hedgerows, and rice paddies. I was on point and had just left a tree line and crossed a rice paddy when a group of automatic weapons (AK 47's) opened up on me. I took cover behind a dike, returned fire, and after a while, the firing stopped. Quickly my fire team linked up with me, but as they came out into the open, the enemy again opened up with their automatic weapons. We returned fire into the tree-line across from the rice paddies. Again, the firing finally stopped. Then the rest of our squad linked up – this time without enemy fire. Our squad leader told me to take my fire team across the rice paddy and check out the snipers' tree-line. I said, 'What! – You want me to take my men out in the open across the rice paddy – directly in the enemy's line of fire?". He said, 'Yes, I know Charlie he hits and runs – they'll be gone.' I said, how about if I take my fire team back into our tree line and follow the tree line around and come up behind them. He said no – he wanted us to go across the rice paddy. I said no. He said that he was giving me a direct order to go, and if I disobeyed a direct order in combat, I would be court-martialed. I again said no but offered again to take my men around the tree-line. He told me to stay where I was, and I was under arrest.

He then called on the radio for the rest of our platoon to link up. Once they were out in the open, close to us, 2 or 3 automatic weapons again opened up on us from the same area. I got in the squad leader's face and said, 'you dumb shit, you would have gotten all of us killed – now let's see who's gonna get court-martialed.' He never said another word about any of that. Technically I suppose I still could have been court-martialed, but nothing was done. This was probably the most significant decision I have made in my life. If I had followed the order, we would have been killed or at least severely wounded. If I would have been wrong and the snipers had left, I could have been court-martialed, which likely would have put me in prison, given me a dishonorable discharge and ruined my life. No-one should have to make those kinds of decisions – least of all a 19-year-old kid. And I can tell you that decision has affected me throughout my life. Whenever I am told to do something that doesn't make sense, I bristle and flashback to that rice paddy and the squad leader. I know the consequences of following wrong orders can be very significant, indeed.

The squad leader gave bad orders and was dangerous. He nearly got me and my fire team killed, and he likely could get other guys killed in the future. And in combat, we took care of our own. We considered what we needed to do about him but ultimately we did not have to do anything because he was moved aside and I was promoted to sergeant and squad leader. As a result we no longer had to follow any of his bad orders.

Back at the newspaper, I continued to be asked to do things that made little sense. I kept telling my boss that I can't function like this. I'm a leader, and I don't need to be crunching numbers on a computer. They should get a young person just out of college to do this stuff. He told me I had little choice, and this is what I had to do. I told him that I did have a choice and that I was strongly considering early retirement at 55.

I could see this likely coming a year or so in advance, so I had applied for my healthcare at the VA, and I got it. One of the main reasons I got it was because of my service-related disability. This is the same one I had unsuccessfully tried to give back. So, the VA became my healthcare. And I started using it and was comfortable with it by the time I took my early retirement at 55. People ask me why I retired so early. I think Vietnam counted for 5 or 10 additional years, so it's not early for me. I recently saw in the mortality tables that the life expectancy for a Vietnam veteran who survived the war is 66...

CHAPTER 9

POINT - A PARATROOPERS MEMOIR OF VIETNAM

After retiring, I had a lot of time to think. The post 9/11 war in Afghanistan had ramped up, and my thoughts kept returning to Vietnam. I had all of these stories in my head about the things that had happened over there. I have always liked to write, so I started writing down the names of these stories. I did this haphazardly at first, just trying to recall the most significant events. Then I put them in chronological order as best as I could remember. I wasn't sure where all of this was going, but I went on and kind of outlined each of these stories. And the last story was me coming home – an end to that horrific nightmare. But I realized that was not the end of Vietnam for me. Not by a long shot.

Vietnam had affected me with my untreated combat fatigue, ultimately morphing into PTSD. And I knew many of us Vietnam vets, especially combat vets, had PTSD. I then decided I would try to write a book, and the last part of it was going to be about my PTSD. I had told few people about my PTSD, fearing people at work would not understand and somehow hold this against me. But I hoped writing about my PTSD experience and how I got help, might prove helpful to others who are suffering and don't know what to do.

I went back to my outlined stories and commenced writing my book. It felt good and cathartic to write down these things that had swirled around in my head and haunted me. Many of the stories I had told my family and therapists about before. And yet writing those down on paper seemed to kind of release their haunting aspects for me, at least to some degree. This felt therapeutic and good. Some of the stories I had not told anyone about. There were other stories that I recalled, but I could not write. They were too horrific and painful. I just wanted them to go away. Other memories were triggered by my writings that

I had blocked out. These were the worst because, as they were recalled, it was like they had just happened. It was like I was back in Vietnam, and these horrible things were happening. Recalling these blocked memories was similar to the APC story triggered by Smitty, as described earlier.

This almost caused me to stop writing. But I had come so far, I was determined to continue. But I needed to protect myself. My book had become a monster that I had created. And what was even scarier was the fact that the manuscript was not really the monster. The monster was within me and my memories.

CHAPTER 10

THE MONSTER BOOK
TURNS ANGELIC

And then I knew what I had to do. I had to go back to the VA for more therapy. My PTSD was roaring inside of me. I was desperate and needed help. So, I went back to the VA and was hooked up with a therapist. I told my therapist about writing my book, which overwhelmed me. She asked me why I undertook such a task without being in therapy. I told her I thought it would be good for me, but now I was going to burn my manuscript because it had hurt me so bad. She said, 'don't burn your manuscript; just leave it aside and do nothing with it as we work through the issues that have been raised. Ultimately, you'll be able to get back to your book, and it will turn into a good thing.' I wondered how that could ever happen, but eventually, she was right. After a year of therapy, I was finally able to get back to my book in a good way. I ended up 'self-publishing' the book through an on-line publishing service. It cost me about $1000 to self-publish the book. Their services included a legal review where they advised me to call the book a novel. This meant the book was fiction but was based on my combat experience in Vietnam. This was important for legal/liability issues, which I didn't totally understand, but I agreed.

I had no idea how many books I would sell and if I would get my money back, but I didn't write the book for money. I felt most people didn't have the slightest idea of what we did in combat during Vietnam. And I thought it was important that they know what we as 18 and 19-year-old teenagers went through and of course the aftermath – PTSD which can last a lifetime.

My book did turn out to be a good thing in many ways. My mother was in a nursing home in and she had a copy of my book on her bed stand. While my second cousin was visiting my mother, he asked about the book. My mom told him that I wrote it, and he got the information so he could purchase the book from Amazon. On the back of the book, I had my e-mail address. So, he sent me an e-mail explaining who he was and how he had seen my book at my mother's. He told me that if he had read my book two years before, his brother would be alive today. He explained that his brother was doing all kinds of dangerous things and was drinking a lot. All of this was out of character for him, and they didn't know what was wrong. He, too, had been a combat veteran in Vietnam. My cousin said it was clear from my book that he had PTSD and needed help from the VA. Had he known, he would have dragged him by the hair, if need be, to get him to the VA. But he did not know, and his brother was killed as he drove off the road drunk and hit a tree.

I also got an e-mail from someone I did not know. He said his brother, too, was a combat veteran in Vietnam and was all messed up. He wouldn't come out of the basement and had been down there for a year. The guy who e-mailed me wanted me to give him a call to talk about his brother. As I spoke with him, he asked what he should do. I told him somehow, he had to get him to the VA. I offered to help. I could come over and talk to him in the basement. Or I could talk to him on the phone. He said no thanks, but I had been very helpful. He would try to get him to the VA. If he needed my help, he would call. The call came many months later. He said his brother was no longer in the basement. I feared he had killed himself. But no, the VA convinced him to come out and see a therapist which he did, and after many, many sessions he was doing better. I said I was so glad, and he thanked me again. He said my book had saved his brother. The monster (my book) had turned angelic...

Another interesting thing happened with my book. My grand-daughter, Maya, was in middle school, and they were about to study the Vietnam War. She asked if I wanted her to tell her teacher I was in the war and had written a book. I said yes and gave Maya a copy of my book for her teacher. Her teacher called me and asked if I would like to give a talk to his class. I had given a couple of talks on my book at church, so I had the materials and said yes. I gave the teacher an outline of what I was going to say, and he said he wanted me to do it. He said the kids would have a lot of questions. And I said that was fine and I felt I could answer just about anything they would ask.

My talk was a summary of my combat experiences beginning when I just got there and was a 'new guy' who was nearly scared to death and just trying to stay alive. My experiences transitioned me to becoming a point man and, ultimately, a seasoned, hardened combat soldier. I spoke of my buddies, some battles, and the triple canopied jungles with all the bazaar animals. I continued telling them about my combat fatigue, my trip home, and my PTSD. I gave this same talk about 5 or 6 times to various schools and classes ranging from the 5th to 9th grade.

The best part of these talks was the kid's questions. One girl asked me if I was afraid. I said, yes. And my experience interacting with other combat vets told me that if they say they weren't afraid, they were either lying or were crazy. We all were afraid, but we did our jobs. She then asked if we were afraid and ran away. I said no, but if there were too many of the enemy, we would pull back and call in artillery (bombs) on them and then go get them. She said that was kind of like running away. I said no, that was kind of like being smart.

One boy asked me if I killed anyone. I said I wasn't sure. We would often have battles in the jungle where it was hard to see the enemy. We shot at them but couldn't necessarily see them. Then after the battle there would be dead enemy soldiers, but we were unsure who had killed them. One time I was shooting a machine gun at two NVA soldiers running out in the open. I was walking the bullets right up to them and had them dead to rights. But suddenly my gun jammed, and they got away. They had no idea how lucky they were. I did not usually carry the machine gun (M60) but our machine gunner complained that he never got to stay back from patrol because we always had to have the machine gun. So, this time I told him I would carry it and he could stay back. He said great, but don't fire it unless you have to as it's a bitch to clean. The reason the machine gun jammed was that I accidentally had my foot on the ammunition belt, which stopped it. He would never have made that mistake, and he would have easily had two kills. And when I got back to our perimeter, he said he had heard me fire the machine gun and asked if I had gotten any kills. I said no, but it was close. I didn't mention the rest…

The kids were fascinated by the animals in the jungle. I told them about when we were back in our fire support base, which was carved out of the jungle. We were on guard duty at night on the perimeter when we heard something in the constantia wire in front of our bunker. We called on the radio to the command post to shine their searchlight in front of our bunker. As the light scanned the wire suddenly, there was a huge Bangle tiger sitting just outside of the wire looking at us. One of my fire team guys raised his weapon to shoot it. I said no, we had to call command. Command told us not to kill the tiger but to throw a rock at it. I said okay, but if it jumps over the wire and comes at us, we will shoot it. So, I threw a rock at it, and it ran away back into the jungle. It had been curious about us. And the command was right; we didn't need to kill the tiger. We sure didn't need a tiger skin rug.

I told them of the Komodo dragons that were about 5 feet tall and would run in an upright position. I told them of the many snakes: pythons, boa constrictors, and the bamboo vipers, also known as two-step snakes. One of our good old boys from Tennessee caught one and was milking the venom out of its fangs on a c- ration can. One of the creepiest things was the centipedes that looked more like millipedes, but much bigger – about 2 to 3 feet long and its body as big around as my forearm. At night sometimes they would crawl over us as we slept on the jungle floor. They often were out at dawn in the jungle. We would take our machetes and hack them into pieces. And each piece would scurry off separately in a different direction back into the jungle.

One girl asked me if my buddies or I was ever hurt by any of these animals in the jungle. I had never thought about this, so at first, I answered no. The animals stayed away from us, and we stayed away from them. Then I hesitated and said two small animals had hurt me in the jungle - leeches and mosquitoes. The leaches were not only in the rivers but also on the damp jungle floors in triple canopy jungles. They really didn't hurt you, but they would attach to you and suck your blood and get big. When we found them, we would squirt mosquito repellant on them, and they would shrivel up and die. The other smaller animal was mosquitoes - namely female anopheles mosquitoes. They transmitted malaria, and I ended up with two types, both of which are recurring.

The questions from the older kids, freshmen, were of a different nature. Many of these questions centered on why we got involved in the war and why we did not win it. We were told we got involved in the war to stop the spread of communism throughout Southeast Asia. North Vietnam was communist and was trying to defeat South Vietnam, a democracy-based country, and bring it under their communist rule. The concern was if North Vietnam won, they might go on into Laos, Cambodia, etc., to further spread their communist influence. This was called the 'domino effect.'

Well, as it turned out, that never happened. North Vietnam was trying to consolidate its country as it was before WWII. North Vietnam had industry but no agriculture. South Vietnam had a lot of rice paddies/food but very little industry. And a lot of the South Vietnamese were North Vietnamese sympathizers – VC (Viet Cong). It was estimated that about ½ of the South Vietnamese Army were VC. And clearly, they did not engage actively in battles against the North Vietnamese or the VC. In the end, we did not defeat North Vietnam. But still, if winning was defined as stopping the spread of communism throughout Southeast Asia, we kind of won as communism went no further than Vietnam. The dominos did not fall...

At many of my talks at schools, they would arrange to have other teachers sit in and listen to me. I received very kind words from the teachers. They told me they had no clue what had gone on over there and thanked me for my service, writing my book, and talking to the kids.

At the VA, my therapist, and some others in the PTSD clinic knew I had written my book, and they asked me to talk to the severe PTSD patients hospitalized at the VA. I asked them if they were sure they wanted me to do this and talk about my Vietnam experience and PTSD. They said absolutely because, despite my PTSD, I had done very well – a good marriage, family, and career. I gave the talk, and it mostly went well, but I got comments somewhat similar to what I had heard in group therapy. One guy saying he was in the Navy and hadn't done anything close to what I had done in Vietnam. He was crying and said he shouldn't be feeling this way. I told him that PTSD was different for everyone. I knew guys that went through way more than me and didn't have PTSD. And some went through far less and had roaring PTSD - way more than me. At least for me, the key to recovery was therapy and having the right therapist and approach. I said I tried group therapy, and I hated it. But individual therapy that included my wife was the key for me. I looked over at the therapists and they were smiling and shaking their heads 'yes'.

CHAPTER 11

VOLUNTEERING AT THE VA

At about this same time, I wore a l73d Airborne tee-shirt to my health club. And someone on one of the elliptical machines said, 'airborne and welcome home brother.' I asked him how he knew about the 173d. He said he had served as a company commander for the 173d in Vietnam. We continued to meet and talk at the health club. He had recently retired, too, and was doing volunteer work at the VA medical center. He told me he worked in 'escort,' pushing patients/vets in wheelchairs and litters (gurneys). He said he liked it and thought I might as well. So, I called the VA and made an appointment to meet with someone from 'voluntary services.' They interviewed me, took my application, and did a background check. They were very thorough, wanting to have the right people to interact with their patients/vets. My application was approved, and I began working in escort. And my friend was right – I did like it a lot. I liked the volunteer work and being around the veterans. And I found out another thing. Sometimes the best way to help your self is by helping others.

In escort, our jobs were basically assistant nursing positions because we had sole responsibility for the patients as we pushed them from one location to another. The medical center and hospital are huge. They say there are about 22 miles of hallways in the facility. When we would go to get a patient, we called the activity a run (patient run). On average, we would do 10 to 12 runs in a 4-hour shift. But if it was busy and we had few volunteers that day, we would barely have time to sit down between runs, and some days we did over 20 runs. The thing that was so interesting about this job was the diversity of the people you had contact with. As far as the veteran patients, they were Army, Navy, Air Force, Marines, and Coast Guard. And their service spanned from WWII to the Afghanistan war and all times in between. And as for the volunteers, most are veterans, with many having their healthcare there at the VA. But many were not veterans, and often these people felt they were serving their country now – volunteering at the VA.

My grand-daughter, Maya, was eight years old when I started volunteering at the VA. Our daughter, Maya's mom, Leslie, was a single mom, so we took care of Maya a lot, especially in the summer. I asked Maya if she wanted to come to the VA with me and help me, volunteer. She said she wasn't sure because sick people made her sad. I said why don't you try it and see how it is. She said, okay. I remember the first patient run we went on. We picked up this lady who was legally blind. I asked her if she wanted to hold my arm to guide her, and she said 'no, she could see enough to follow Maya in her pretty bright red dress.' So, we took her to her destination, and she thanked us and hugged Maya. As we went back to escort (our escort volunteer room), I asked Maya how she liked that. She said she liked it a lot. It felt so good to help someone like that. Maya was hooked.

Well, the patients became hooked on Maya as well. There are not many kids around the VA, and very few pretty, little, sweet girls like Maya. When we went to pick up a patient, they would say, 'I see you have a little helper today.' They were thrilled to have Maya come along. So, during the summers, Maya came with me almost every time I volunteered, which initially was three days a week, but then I cut back to two days.

Maya did this from the time she was eight until she was 14. Mostly we worked escort but also sometimes we worked at the information center with another volunteer, an ex-Navy guy who was very funny. We had a great time.

When Maya was in middle school, they had a trip to Washington, DC. There was an opportunity for four of the students on the trip to lay a wreath at the tomb of the unknowns. Those students wanting to lay the wreath had to write an essay as to why they wanted to do it. Maya wrote about me being a paratrooper in Vietnam and her and me volunteering at the VA. She also wrote how important it is to honor the Vets for all they have done for us. Maya was selected, and I had her wear my 173d insignia pin on her dress for the ceremony. Maya was so honored to be able to do this. And we were all so proud of her.

At 14, Maya became an official student volunteer working escort some, but she also served free coffee to the vets as she pushed a coffee cart around the medical center. One summer, she had a friend who joined her volunteering at the VA. We would pick up Maya's friend, and off we would go to the VA.

CHAPTER 12

THE VOLUNTEERS

There are a wide variety of volunteers at the VA. Most tend to be veterans, many of which have their health care at the VA. Others are not veterans, and when I ask if they had served, they often would respond in an apologetic tone and say 'no, they had not served but wished they had.' When I heard this, I would say, 'well you are serving your country now and not even getting paid for it.' And I believe that is true. As volunteers, we help our country meet our commitment to providing health care to those who have served with honor.

Right from the beginning, I was very impressed by a couple of WWII combat vets volunteering with us. One was Frank, and the other was Arnie. Neither of them talked too much about their combat. Arnie was an infantry guy who was assigned to a tank company. Most often, tanks have infantry with them to make for a more formidable fighting force when engaged in combat. Frank told us he was just an 18-year-old kid who they told to get down in the tank and to load shells in the tank gun after it was fired. He said he could not see what was going on but knew, at times, they were involved in fierce battles as he continued loading shells, round after round, into the tank gun.

Frank told us of one of the most disturbing events that he witnessed. They had managed to capture a Nazi train. As it turned out, this train was headed to the death camps. The people who came walking out of that train were like walking skeletons – absolutely unbelievable. Frank told us if we ever encountered someone who did not believe in the holocaust, we should tell them to talk to him. The inhumanity and horror of it all was scarred into Frank's brain at a tender age of 18. When people say 'war is hell' they don't know the half of it.

Unfortunately Frank and Arnie have passed now. And like so many of our other WWII vets, America has lost some of her best.

Phil, another volunteer, was a Navy pilot in the early 1960s. He flew a sub-chaser, which was a plane designed to track Russian submarines during the cold war. Phil was in the south Pacific when they were testing nuclear weapons. Although hard to believe, they had Phil fly his airplane through a nuclear mushroom cloud. They had affixed a dosimeter to his uniform that recorded the amount of radiation he had been exposed to. I asked him if he considered saying no. He said, 'you know, Rick, – we couldn't say no.' I asked him if they decontaminated him. He said, 'No, but they did my plane.'

Phil had real bad skin cancer, so I asked him if he filed a disability claim with the VA being he had been exposed to nuclear radiation. He said no, the doctors here at the VA said it was from the sun. I said, 'bullshit, they can't have you fly your plane through a mushroom cloud and then say your cancer is from the sun'.

Phil lived in the same county as me, so I took him to my veteran service officer to file a claim. I introduced Phil to him and briefly told him about the mushroom cloud. He was astonished and thanked me for bringing Phil to him. He took Phil into his office and closed the door. When Phil came out, he said the veteran service officer was filing a claim, and he was all but positive that Phil would be awarded something.

And, as it turned out, the veteran service officer was right. Initially, he was awarded a 30% disability, and later it was increased to 40% which included monthly monetary payments. As the VA investigated this, they were able to turn up the record of the dosimeter readings showing how much radiation

Phil had been exposed to. Phil didn't have much money, so he was very thankful to me for helping him get this. He hugged me and was crying. He said his daughters were grateful to me as well. How the Navy could do that to Phil or anyone else is beyond me. Unfortunately, Phil passed away a couple of years ago.

One marine who volunteered with us knew I saw a lot of combat in Vietnam, including being a point man, and he asked me, 'if you were so gung-ho, why didn't you join the Marines?' I said, 'it's simple – I wanted to be a paratrooper."

One of the most legendary volunteers we had was another former Marine who had been a sniper. He is a great guy. He not only volunteered at escort, but he also volunteered for the Military Order of the Purple Heart. He was a member of that organization having received a purple heart in Vietnam. In fact, he was wounded twice in one battle, but somehow, they only counted that as one Purple Heart.

We became great friends as we not only shared similar combat experience – he as a Marine and me as an Army paratrooper, but we also had severe, chronic PTSD. At times when we would be having PTSD trouble and couldn't get to see our therapists, we would talk to each other. And it helped immensely maybe even more than with a therapist.

I'm not sure how many confirmed kills he had as a sniper, but it was far more than a couple. He told of the time he had climbed up in a palm tree and was sniping the Viet Cong (VC) from up there. They couldn't figure out where he was at. But they got reinforcements and attacked his platoon. The platoon leader called for them to pull back, leaving him up in the tree all by himself. He stayed up there until night-time when he climbed down and snuck back through the enemy to his platoon. He had some serious words with that rookie platoon leader. He was a legend and the platoon leader was a green 2nd lieutenant. Needless to say, that platoon leader stayed well clear of him after their little discussion.

A few years back, they had a study and gave guys with severe PTSD brain scans to see if there was a difference in the PTSD brains vs. others. Three of us from escort had the scans, and we also had the option of being informed if they found anything else during the brain scans. They found an old TBI (traumatic brain injury/brain bleed) in the marine sniper's scan; they figured it happened about the time he was in Vietnam. He said one time he was riding on a tank when the tank hit a booby-trapped artillery round. It blew him off the tank and knocked him out for about 10 minutes. When he woke up, the squad leader asked if he was all right. He said he had a bad headache. The squad leader said, 'okay – let's go.'

The marine sniper was only awarded one Purple Heart, but he should have had three. Two from being wounded twice in the same firefight (shot by an AK47 in the shoulder & shrapnel in his back) and another from his TBI/brain bleed when he was blown off the tank.

And we were given the overall results of the brain scans. They found there was a discernable difference in the PTSD brain scans vs. others. This was a significant finding as it clearly showed a definite physical difference in severe PTSD patients' brains.

The marine sniper liked my grand-daughter, Maya, a lot. Surely it was because Maya was such a sweet, nice little girl and a volunteer to boot. Anyway, the feeling was mutual, and Maya liked him a bunch as well. And as a token of their friendship, he gave Maya one of his prized Marine caps, which she proudly wore around the VA at times.

Maya got involved in musical theatre in middle school – singing solos, dancing, and acting. Almost from the get-go, he would come and see Maya perform. And he would always be wearing his marine jacket and marine hat – like they say 'once a marine, always a marine'. Maya and our whole family were thrilled to have him there. Maya's performances continued throughout high school, and college and his attendance did likewise as did their close friendship.

CHAPTER 13

THE VETERANS

One great thing about working escort is getting to meet and talk with the vets that we are transporting. I always ask the vets what branch of the service they had been in. I heard it all – Army, Navy, Marines, Air Force, Coast Guard, and even Merchant Marines. During my first week working escort, I picked up a lady, and I asked her if she was a veteran. She said, 'why the Hell else would I be here getting my health care.' I said I was sorry for asking, and I never made that rookie mistake again. However, I have escorted women who had their healthcare at the VA because their husbands had been 100% disabled and had died from their disability. This opened up the VA to the surviving spouse for health care irrespective of whether they were veterans or not.

Generally, I found that most of the vets liked talking about their service. They are proud of it and seldom had an opportunity to talk about it. After asking what branch they had served in, I generally would ask where they were stationed and what they did in the service. I met a guy who was on one of the 1st ships torpedoed in Pearl Harbor (the West Virginia). And he said eight torpedoes later they sunk. Coincidently, a week later I was pushing another guy who said he was on the West Virginia in WWII. I asked if he was on it when it sank at Pearl Harbor. He said no, but they refloated her, fixed her up, and then took her to battle in the Pacific.

I also met guys who served with Patton in WWII. They said he really had the pearl-handled 45's and was a real 'rah-rah' kind of guy who said 'we are going to kick the sons of bitches German asses.' And after Vietnam, I actually saw those 45's at the Patton Museum when I was stationed at Fort Knox – the armor center. I've read books about Patton, who, in my opinion, was one of our best generals in WWII. At one point, the 101ˢAirborne was surrounded at Bastogne. Eisenhower called together his top generals and asked who could save the 101ˢᵗ. A couple of generals said it would take two divisions and at least two months. Patton said he could do it with one division, and it would take two weeks. Ike told Patton to do it. Patton did do it with one division, and he did it in 1 week.

WWII vets are pretty much gone now, but a couple of years ago, I pushed a real old guy on a litter, and I asked him what branch of the service he was in. He said the Navy a long, long time ago. I wondered if it was in WWII. He said yes. I asked him what kind of a ship he was on. He said he couldn't remember. I asked him what he did on the ship. He said he was a deck gunner and shot down Kami Kazzis. He said that they just kept coming at their ship, and he kept shooting down those sons of bitches. I thought he must have been a good shot because he and his ship had survived.

Another WWII guy that I met had made five combat paratroop jumps during WWII. How he survived all of that is beyond me. These WWII vets literally saved the world.

I met all kinds of Vietnam veterans who I could relate to. I'd ask them where they were located, what unit they were with, and what they did over there. I knew a lot about Vietnam and many of the units that served. So, we had good talks. Some guys didn't want to talk about it at all. They were probably suffering from PTSD. But if they said they didn't want to talk; I would just shut up and say no more.

One time I was pushing a guy from the 5ᵗʰ Infantry Division in Vietnam. I told him I was with the 173d, and he asked me if I did the only combat jump in Vietnam at operation Junction City. I said no that was in 1966, and I served mostly in 1968.

He said he was there as the 5th infantry provided security for the drop zone. I had heard before that there was a serious question about whether this had really been a combat jump, and I told him this. I told him that they started up a jumpmaster school in An Khe, which I attended, and that we did three training jumps outside the base camp without drop zone security. One could say our jumps were as much or more combat jumps than Junction City. But in reality none of them were even close.

I was pushing one Vietnam veteran, and he was kind of delirious and kept saying, 'the snakes, the snakes, they were horrible.' I asked him what about the snakes. He said he was with the 'Graves Registration Unit.' They would go to battlefields to recover our dead soldier's bodies and dog tags. He went to one battlefield where there were reported numerous dead American soldiers. When he got there, he could not find any, but he found several boa constrictors with large lumps in their bodies. He killed one and slit it open only to find a dead American soldier. He hated to do more, but he had to recover as many as possible, which he did. He said he has never been the same ever since. Horrific PTSD in spades...

This VA became a designated traumatic brain injury (TBI) center to treat Iraq and Afghanistan war-wounded with TBI. It was unfortunate to see how many of our soldiers had been hurt so badly. Many of these patients were on litters and were unconscious. And yet, despite the severity of these injuries, many of these patients improved significantly. I remember one in particular who was conscious but unable to speak. When we asked him a question, all he could do was a thumbs-up or thumbs-down. I still see the 'thumbs-up/down' Marine who now talks and walks with a cane. I was at a major league baseball game, and they had this same Marine throw out the first pitch. He was in his dress blue uniform and was pushed out to the pitching mound in a wheelchair. He stood up, saluted, and threw the pitch as best he could and then gave a thumbs-up. The crowd roared their appreciation of his service and sacrifice,

I pushed another young Army paratrooper who had an 82nd Airborne hat on his litter. His girlfriend or wife was with him. He was a triple amputee – two legs and an arm. I greeted him by saying 'Airborne', and he responded with 'all the way' (a typical greeting for fellow paratroopers). Once we got to where his appointment was, he asked me what unit I had been with, and I said 'the 173d in Vietnam.' He shook my hand and said, 'thanks for your service.' And I thanked him for his and quickly left as I did not want him to see the tears streaming down my face.

One thing about volunteering at the VA, we see veterans who are in very bad shape. And it makes us feel thankful for what we have as opposed to feeling sorry for our relatively minor aches and pains. Assisting these proud veterans makes us feel honored to be of help. And in helping others, we help ourselves. There has been talk of trying to outsource more veterans' healthcare into the community's health services. I think that would be a huge mistake. There is so much camaraderie between vets in these VA facilities. There is a physical aspect of getting well, but there is a psychological part of it also. The psychological benefit of being surrounded by veterans and being treated by health care professionals who understand veterans, all of this is healing in a very unique way. Veterans can never get this type of healing out in the community.

CHAPTER 14

HEALTH CARE AT THE VA

I have had my health care at the VA since I took early retirement at the age of 55 – 16 years ago. I have had numerous orthopedic issues. I've had both of my big toe joints fused, both knees replaced, both hips replaced, and my lower back is a mess. The chief orthopedic surgeon at the VA was talking to me about all of this. He knew I had been a paratrooper, and he asked how many jumps I had made. I told him only eight, but I had a nasty landing on one of them, and two instructors came running up to me & told me not even to try to get up because I had broken both of my legs. Well, they were wrong as I commenced to get up and walk away – unhurt. But I told him that we did combat assaults out of Huey helicopters in Vietnam. The helicopters wouldn't land as they were afraid of getting shot down. At about 5 or 10 feet, they would flare and hover for a few seconds as we jumped off the struts with 65-pound packs on our backs plus our M16's, ammunition, hand grenades, etc. He asked me how many of those did I do. I said easily 40 or 50. He said, 'make no mistake about it. Each of those severely compressed every weight-bearing joint in your body. When you're 18 or 19 years old, it doesn't necessarily hurt you then, but the damage was done, and later in life, it shows up. Mostly these surgeries have gone well and have helped me a lot.

When I was 60 years old, I was mowing my back yard, which had a big hill. As I was going down the hill, I stepped on a big mushroom, which was slippery. My feet slipped, and when they caught, I fell on my knees and was falling into my lawnmower. I then threw myself back and ended up flat on my back with my knees bent totally under me. I couldn't get up – my knees wouldn't work. I scooted back up the hill, went inside our 4-season porch, called my wife's cell phone, and told her I was hurt. We had a pair of crutches in the garage, so she got them, and I tried 'walking it off.' It did not work, and I fell twice, hurting my knees even more. After the second fall, Judy got our neighbor who helped me up into a chair, and we called 911. The police came first, and they were worried that I was going into shock. The paramedics arrived and got me on a gurney and into the ambulance. They asked me where I wanted to go, and I said to the VA, but I didn't think they accepted ambulance patients. They said that they had changed a few months before. So, they called the VA, and the VA said he's one of ours bring him in.

They took me into the emergency room, and an ER doctor took one look at my knees, and he said, 'oh my God, I think you have dislocated both of your knees.' I'm getting an orthopedic doctor right now. They brought in a resident who commenced to do a routine examination of my knees. But as she bent my knee, I screamed out in pain, and she said I think you are hurt really bad. I'm getting one of the staff surgeons who just got out of surgery. This other doctor looked at my knees and pressed his fingertips into my knees just above my kneecaps. Again, I screamed in pain. He said I had severed both of my quadriceps tendons, and I needed emergency surgery; otherwise, my quadriceps muscles would die. They put my legs in braces so my knees couldn't bend and took me to a hospital ward. They had a commode next to my bed, and they showed me how I could use a board to transfer (slide) onto the commode and also into my wheel chair. I had the surgery, which went well, and I had casts on both of my legs from my groin to toes. They then told me I would have to be non-weight bearing in a wheelchair for at least three months.

Mostly I was doing well, and the surgeons would come to see me every morning. They came in my room is a specific order with the chief orthopedic surgeon in the lead, followed by the staff surgeon who had done my surgery, and bringing up the rear was the orthopedic surgical resident. The only person who spoke was the chief surgeon who asked me some questions and told me how I was doing. The others were silent. There was definitely a chain of command there. He told me that after a couple of weeks, I could possibly go home.

I could transfer from my bed, using the board, to my wheelchair, which had leg rests sticking straight out in the front. I was encouraged to go to the patient dining room for meals when I felt good enough. I ate in my room at first, but after a week or so, I ate most of my meals in the dining room.

My physical therapist encouraged me so much. With my legs in casts, there wasn't much therapy to be done, but she was impressed by my upper body strength, and she helped me maintain that as it would prove helpful to my recovery. And she was right. One time two young nurses tried to pick me up out of my hospital bed to transfer me to my wheelchair. I had a hold of the steel triangle that was hung over my bed when they dropped me. But I did not hit the floor. I pulled myself back up on the bed and told them I was okay but to get someone bigger and stronger.

After 3½ weeks, my surgeon told me that, medically speaking, I was okay to go home. He asked me if I had someone at home who could help me. I said my wife works from home and that she could. He said the VA could arrange to have ramps built in front of my house to have wheelchair access into my home. They would also put a hospital bed in my living room and a commode as well. They would send care cabs to pick me up and take me to and from the VA to see my surgeons and my therapist. Or, he said, I will keep you in this ward until I could walk out of there. I asked how long that would be. He said three months. I told him I wanted to go home.

The VA made arrangements to do all the things that my surgeon talked about. They built the ramps, which were like aluminum dock sections. They fit them together for me, and then when I no longer needed them, they took them apart for use by someone else. They also put the hospital bed and commode in my living room. Once all of that was complete, they had an occupational therapist go to my house and inspect it to ensure everything was okay and safe for me.

I remember the care cab ride from the hospital that took me home. The driver pushed me up the ramps into the living room, and I was home. At home, I could wheel myself out of the living room into the dining room and kitchen. That was it, but it sure was better than the hospital ward.

Finally, after about three months, my surgeon said it was time for me to start walking again with the braces at first. They removed my casts, and I was shocked to see my legs. They were nothing but skin and bone. All my muscles had totally atrophied. And a lot of the skin was dead skin from being in the casts so long.

They cleaned up my legs, put my braces on, and took me to therapy. My physical therapist told me that we (her and I) were going to walk with the parallel bars. She said she didn't care how strong I was or that I had been a paratrooper. This was going to be scary and one of the hardest things I've done in my life. They wheeled me to the parallel bars and stood me up with my hands on the bars. At the same time, my therapist was in front of me, facing me, and she wrapped her arms around me, giving me a bear hug. There were two other therapists, one on each side of me to make sure I didn't fall. She said, 'let's go, one step at a time.' And we went, shaky, slowly, and haltingly. But we went to the end of the bars. They sat me down in my wheelchair. I had done it. And all three therapists applauded for me.

She asked me how that was. I said, can you imagine how scared I was when I stood in the airplane door for my first parachute jump? Well, this was worse. But I said to her 'at least we were kind of dancing'. She laughed and asked if I'd come back tomorrow and dance again. I said I didn't want to, but I would.

With my therapist's help, I progressed from the parallel bars to a walker. She also loosened my braces a little at a time to allow some knee bend. And she was relentless in getting me to bend my knees more and more as they had been immobile for more than three months and could freeze up if we did not get the proper knee bend. Ultimately as I improved with my walker, I did not need my wheelchair anymore. My wife, Judy, could take me back and forth in the car to the VA. I could use a wheelchair there, given the long hallways.

So, the worst of my ordeal was over. The VA had fixed me, and they told me that my injury was so severe, that given my age, I was lucky to have walked again. It was the VA, my surgeon and my therapist that had helped me to walk again. Luck had very little to do with it. Anyway, the VA took away my hospital bed, commode, and the ramps. As I think back on it, if this had been a private hospital, my bill would have easily been well over $1 million, and I would have lost my insurance. My cost to the VA was 0, and my healthcare continued unfazed.

A couple of years ago, I was having significant orthopedic issues. I had watched the 10-part CNN documentary on

Vietnam. The documentary portrayed the untruths our government had told the American people about Vietnam.

They knew we could not win the war the way it was being fought, but they continued - killing nearly 58000 of my brothers in arms. I kind of knew some of this before, but this documentary absolutely confirmed it, and it devastated me. I felt betrayed and that my country had abandoned all my Vietnam buddies and me. And with my PTSD and all of my orthopedic issues stemming from Vietnam, I felt that Vietnam had ruined my life -unnecessarily.

I talked to my therapist about this, and he said, 'so Vietnam has ruined your life'? I said yes. He then asked if I was married, and I said yes. He wondered how many times, and I said once. He asked how many years and I said 50. Any adult children? I said, yes. Do your children love you, and are they involved in your lives? I said, yes. Did you have a good job/career? I said yes, but my PTSD caused me to be forced into early retirement at the age of 55. He asked if that had placed a financial burden on me. I said no my VA disability had helped immensely. He asked if I had ever been in trouble with the law. I said no. He asked if I had just listened to what I had said. He said, 'Vietnam did not ruin your life. You have had a good life. Vietnam has complicated your life with PTSD and all of your orthopedic issues. You have dealt well with your PTSD, and you and the VA are trying to work through the orthopedic stuff which granted has been very significant'.

I said I hadn't been able to do hardly anything for the past two years. We had to cancel our Alaskan cruise for our 50th wedding anniversary because I could have only gone in a wheelchair. I said I hadn't played golf in two years and felt I never would golf again. My therapist said he was a golfer and would be devastated not to be able to golf. But he said he would not give it up and would do everything he could to get back to it again. He said if I felt I never would golf again – I wouldn't. But if you tell yourself that you could golf again – you might. Don't give up.

This was about a year ago. And after having not golfed for nearly three years, I did play nine holes of golf a couple of weeks ago. I amazed myself by hitting the ball well. Not far but well. A start, and now I know I can do it at least to some degree. This is another example of the VA continuing to help me and encouraging me to do better. But make no mistake, Vietnam hurt me significantly and it continues to do so.

Over the 15 plus years, I have been escorting vets. I always ask them how they are being taken care of. Well over 9 out of 10 responses have been great or very good. They feel their treatment has been excellent, and the healthcare workers have been fantastic – treating them as vets with honor and respect. And of course, the camaraderie of being around other vets has been tremendous and healing of itself.

At one point, the government had sent inspectors into the Veterans Home – a separate nursing home for vets not far from our VA. If you send inspectors into any nursing home, there will be many, many transgressions. Well, this Vet Home was no exception. There were numerous problems pointed out, and because this was the VA, this story made headlines in our newspaper. It seems negative stories about the VA almost always get highly publicized. In fact, that is one of the reasons I decided to write this memoir. There are at least ten things right about the VA to one wrong thing. But of course, the one thing wrong gets headlines whereas the ten things right go unnoticed.

At about the same time, the inspector's findings were all over the news. I saw a shuttle arrive from the Vets Home – bringing residents to the medical center for their health care. I asked a couple of them how their care was at the Vets Home. Both said it was great and that the vets love it over there.

One of the best things about our VA is its one-stop shopping. Within the VA Medical Center, you have your primary care, specialty care (orthopedic, dermatology, eye clinic, audiology, prosthetics, x-ray, CT scans, MRI's, physical therapy, etc.), hospital wards, intensive care, hospice, surgery, pharmacy, oncology, mental health, etc. The medical center also has a cafeteria.

As far as my medications, I can get refills through the mail by either calling them in or using the VA patient website, My Healthy Vet. And when I see one of my doctors, and they write me a prescription, I can go to the pharmacy, talk to a pharmacist, and get my medication usually within 20 to 30 minutes. I can also use My Healthy Vet to send secure messages (e-mails) to my doctors and get answers within a couple of days.

Sometimes it may take two or three weeks to get an appointment. But if you have a more urgent need, you can call a triage nurse who will consider your situation and can get you in to see someone within a day or so if the need is urgent. There have been times when I was at the VA for my volunteer work, and I needed to see someone in a specialty clinic. I have walked up to the clinic and have told the receptionist what was going on. When the need has been somewhat urgent, on occasion, I have been told to sit in the waiting room, and they would squeeze me in, which they did.

Our VA has been consistently rated as one of the top 5 in the country – so we are very fortunate. Although the VA's healthcare is not perfect, it is very, very good. No healthcare system is perfect. And of course the bureaucracy is alive and well. But speaking for myself and for so many other vets I have talked with, we are very happy with the VA despite its imperfections, and we are very thankful to have it.

THE END

Printed in the United States
by Baker & Taylor Publisher Services